the
ROMANS

by Colin Hynson
Consultant: Dr. Isabella Sandwell

How to use this book

Each topic in this book is clearly labelled and contains all these components:

Topic heading

Introduction to the topic

Sub-topic 1 offers complete information about one aspect of the topic

Words in capitals are explained in the Glossary

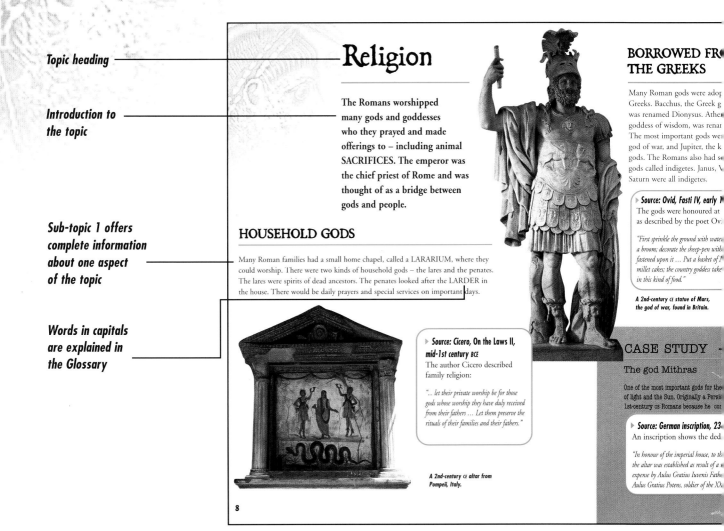

Religion

The Romans worshipped many gods and goddesses who they prayed and made offerings to – including animal SACRIFICES. The emperor was the chief priest of Rome and was thought of as a bridge between gods and people.

HOUSEHOLD GODS

Many Roman families had a small home chapel, called a LARARIUM, where they could worship. There were two kinds of household gods – the lares and the penates. The lares were spirits of dead ancestors. The penates looked after the LARDER in the house. There would be daily prayers and special services on important days.

▶ **Source: Cicero, On the Laws II, mid-1st century BCE**
The author Cicero described family religion:

"... let their private worship be for those gods whose worship they have duly received from their fathers ... Let them preserve the rituals of their families and their fathers."

A 2nd-century CE altar from Pompeii, Italy.

BORROWED FR◆ THE GREEKS

Many Roman gods were adop Greeks. Bacchus, the Greek g was renamed Dionysus. Athe goddess of wisdom, was renar The most important gods we god of war, and Jupiter, the k gods. The Romans also had se gods called indigetes. Janus, \ Saturn were all indigetes.

▶ **Source: Ovid, Fasti IV, early I**
The gods were honoured at as described by the poet Ov

"First sprinkle the ground with wate a broom; decorate the sheep-pen with fastened upon it ... Put a basket of I millet cakes; the country goddess take in this kind of food."

A 2nd-century CE statue of Mars, the god of war, found in Britain.

CASE STUDY

The god Mithras

One of the most important gods for the of light and the Sun. Originally a Persia 1st-century CE Romans because he cor

▶ **Source: German inscription, 23◆**
An inscription shows the ded

"In honour of the imperial house, to th the altar was established as result of a ◆ expense by Aulus Gratius Iuvenis Fathe Aulus Gratius Potens, soldier of the XX◆

8

ISBN 978 1 84898 078 5

This edition published in 2009 by *ticktock* Media Ltd

Printed in China

9 8 7 6 5 4 3 2 1

A CIP catalogue record for this book is available from the British Library.

Copyright © *ticktock* Entertainment Ltd 2005. First published in Great Britain in 2005 by *ticktock* Media Ltd, The Old Sawmill, 103 Goods Station Road, Tunbridge Wells, Kent, TN1 2DP.

Sub-topic 2 offers complete information
about one aspect of the topic

Some suggested words
to use in your project

The Glossary
explains the
meaning of any
unusual or
difficult words
appearing on
these two pages

Words to use in your project

ceremony – a formal occasion celebrating an important event
deity – a god or goddess
immortal – living forever, like the gods
pious – very religious
polytheism – the belief in many gods

Glossary

larder – a cupboard for storing food
lararium – a place in a house where a Roman family would worship
millet – a cereal plant
sacrifice – things killed as offerings to the gods

Other pages in the
book that relate to
what you have read
here are listed
in this bar

See also: The Roman Army 14–15; Death and Burial 16–17;
Living at Home 28–29; Pastimes 30–31

The Case Study
is a closer look
at a famous
person, artefact
or building
that relates
to the topic

.thras, the god
led to the
disorder.

.lithras
.wn
.s) and

A 3rd-century CE relief from
Rome of the god Mithras.

9

Captions clearly
explain what is
in the picture

Each photo or illustration is
described and discussed in its
accompanying text

CONTENTS

Creation of the Roman Empire

The Italian city of Rome was once ruled by kings. But in 509 BCE, King Tarquin the Proud was driven out and Rome became a REPUBLIC. From then on, Rome began to conquer its neighbours. The Roman EMPIRE grew across Europe, North Africa and Asia.

WHERE WAS THE ROMAN EMPIRE?

Soon after becoming a republic, Rome took control of Italy and the Mediterranean.

A few hundred years later, the Romans conquered other lands. This included Spain in 197 BCE, and Gaul (modern France), Turkey, Syria, Egypt, Israel and Jordan between 58 and 50 BCE.

▶ **Source: Herodian, History of the Emperors, VII.iii. 1, 3rd century CE**

Roman writers such as Herodian and Cassius Dio described the empire's conquests:

"What was the use of destroying BARBARIANS, when the killing in Rome itself and the provinces subject to her was on a larger scale? What was the use of seizing booty from the enemy only to be stripped naked oneself and see one's relatives deprived of their property? An invitation had been given to informers to do their DASTARDLY work with complete license."

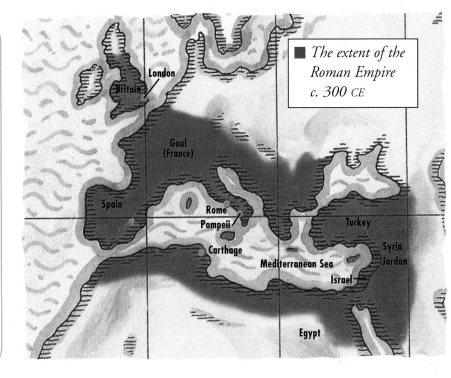

■ *The extent of the Roman Empire c. 300 CE*

This map shows the Roman Empire, under Emperor Trajan, in the 2nd century CE.

WHEN DID THE ROMAN EMPIRE EXIST?

According to Roman MYTHOLOGY, Rome was founded in 753 BCE by twin brothers Romulus and Remus. They were the sons of Mars, the god of war. When they were babies, their uncle put them in the River Tiber to drown, but they were rescued by a wolf. When they grew up, they killed their uncle and built the city of Rome.

A carving of the twin brothers Romulus and Remus from the 2nd century CE.

> ▶ **Source: Cicero, On the Republic, Vol V, mid-1st century BCE**
> The author Cicero described Rome's beginnings:
>
> *"Consequently it seems to me that Romulus must at the very beginning have had a DIVINE INTIMATION that the city would one day be the seat and hearthstone of a mighty empire; for scarcely could a city placed upon any other site in Italy have more easily maintained our present widespread DOMINION."*

Words to use in your project

campaign – a course of action to achieve a particular goal

civilization – a structured society

deposed – thrown out of power

monarch – a king or queen

occupy – to take control of a place through military conquest

prosper – to succeed; flourish

subdue – to weaken

vanquish – to conquer

Glossary

barbarians – people without a structured society

BCE – before the Common Era

CE – Common Era

dastardly – wicked and cruel

divine intimation – a religious or psychic vision

dominion – a land ruled by its own people (rather than a king)

empire – many states ruled over by a single state or king

mythology – a collection of traditional stories or beliefs

republic – a country ruled by a small group rather than one person

sovereignty – supreme power or authority

See also: Rulers and Ruled 6–7; Travel and Trade 12–13; The Roman Army 14–15; Buildings and Engineering 18–19

CASE STUDY

Conquering Britain

Britain became part of the Roman world in 55 BCE when Julius Caesar landed an army in Kent. The Romans arrived again in 43 CE, but it took another 35 years before Britain was conquered.

> ▶ **Source: Corpus Inscriptionum Latinarum, Vol VI No 920, mid-1st century CE**
> An inscription records the victory of Claudius over Britain:
>
> *"… he received the surrender of eleven kings of Britain conquered without reverse and because he was the first to subject to the SOVEREIGNTY of the Roman people …"*

This bronze bust of Claudius is from the 1st century CE.

Rulers and Ruled

At the top of Roman society was the emperor, followed by CONSULS who managed the SENATE and SENATORS who made the laws. Ordinary people were divided into citizens and non-citizens. At the bottom were the slaves.

BREAKING THE LAW

In the early days of Rome, the 12 Tables were created. These provided the basis for law and order over the next 1,000 years. Anybody who broke the law had to face the local judge, or PRAETOR. The most powerful praetors were the regional governors of the Roman Empire. Only the emperor was more powerful than them.

A 1st-century bronze figurine of a praetor.

This Italian coffin made in 270 CE shows members of the Roman senate.

▶ **Source: Juvenal, Satire 8.88–91, late 1st–early 2nd century BCE**

Roman officials were often described as corrupt, as suggested in a passage from one of Juvenal's *Satires*:

"When at last the province to which you have long looked forward receives you as governor, put a rein and CURB on your anger, and on your greed; take some pity on the poor PROVINCIALS, keep in mind what the law PRESCRIBES, what the senate lies down."

ROME'S LAWMAKERS

The senate was a group that represented the people and its members were elected by Roman citizens. The senate was responsible for making laws. Before the Romans had emperors, the senate was the most important organization in the empire. Under the emperors it acted as an advisor and a court of law. Authors such as Tacitus wrote about the way the senators flattered the emperor.

> ▶ **Source: Tacitus, Annals III. 64, late 1st century CE**
> According to Tacitus, Emperor Tiberius described the senators as:
>
> *"men fit to be slaves"*
>
> This is because he thought they grovelled around the emporers in the way slaves served their masters.

Words to use in your project

assassinate – *to kill a political or religious leader*
corruption – *dishonest or illegal behaviour*
democracy – *a state where citizens have a say in the government*
erupt – *to break out suddenly*
magistrate – *a judge*
ruthless – *having no pity*
stability – *a state of being that is not changed easily*

Glossary

consuls – *the top Roman judges*
curb – *to hold back*
praetor – *a Roman judge*
prescribes – *asks or recommends*
provincials – *people who live in states of a country or empire*
senate – *an assembly of important Romans who made laws and advised the rulers of Rome*
senators – *men elected by citizens to join the Roman senate*

See also: Creation of the Roman Empire 4–5; Writing 10–11; Gladiators 20–21

CASE STUDY

Emperor Augustus

For hundreds of years, Rome was a republic, governed by generals who fought one another for control. One general named Julius Caesar ruled Rome but was murdered in 44 BCE. Caesar's adopted son, Augustus, restored order and was declared the first emperor of Rome in 27 BCE. He ruled until his death in 14 CE.

> ▶ **Source: Augustus, Res Gestae, late 1st century BCE**
> Emperor Augustus wrote about himself in *Res Gestae*. This boastful document describes:
>
> *"The achievements of the divine Augustus by which he brought the world under the empire of the Roman people and the expenses which he bore for the state and people of Rome."*

This marble statue of Emperor Augustus was made around 63 BCE and comes from Velletri, Italy.

Religion

The Romans worshipped many gods and goddesses who they prayed and made offerings to – including animal SACRIFICES. The emperor was the chief priest of Rome and was thought of as a bridge between gods and people.

HOUSEHOLD GODS

Many Roman families had a small home chapel, called a LARARIUM, where they could worship. There were two kinds of household gods – the lares and the penates. The lares were spirits of dead ancestors. The penates looked after the LARDER in the house. There would be daily prayers and special services on important days.

▸ **Source: Cicero, On the Laws II, mid-1st century BCE**

The author Cicero described family religion:

"… let their private worship be for those gods whose worship they have duly received from their fathers … Let them preserve the rituals of their families and their fathers."

A 2nd-century CE altar from Pompeii, Italy.

BORROWED FROM THE GREEKS

Many Roman gods were adopted from the Greeks. Bacchus, the Greek god of wine, was renamed Dionysus. Athena, the Greek goddess of wisdom, was renamed Minerva. The most important gods were Mars, the god of war, and Jupiter, the king of the gods. The Romans also had some original gods called indigetes. Janus, Vesta and Saturn were all indigetes.

> ▶ **Source: Ovid, Fasti IV, early 1st century BCE**
>
> The gods were honoured at festivals, as described by the poet Ovid:
>
> *"First sprinkle the ground with water and sweep it with a broom; decorate the sheep-pen with leaves and branches fastened upon it … Put a basket of MILLET with the millet cakes; the country goddess takes special pleasure in this kind of food."*

A 2nd-century CE statue of Mars, the god of war, found in Britain.

Words to use in your project

ceremony – *a formal occasion celebrating an important event*
deity – *a god or goddess*
immortal – *living forever, like the gods*
pious – *very religious*
polytheism – *the belief in many gods*

Glossary

lararium – *a place in a house where a Roman family would worship*
larder – *a cupboard for storing food*
millet – *a cereal plant*
sacrifices – *things killed as offerings to the gods*

See also: The Roman Army 14–15; Death and Burial 16–17; Living at Home 28–29; Pastimes 30–31

CASE STUDY

The god Mithras

One of the most important gods for the Roman army was Mithras, the god of light and the Sun. Originally a Persian god, Mithras appealed to the 1st-century CE Romans because he conquered darkness and disorder.

> ▶ **Source: German inscription, 236 CE**
>
> An inscription shows the dedication to Mithras:
>
> *"In honour of the imperial house, to the unconquerable god Mithras the altar was established as result of a vow to the god at their own expense by Aulus Gratius Iuvenis Father of the rites (of Mithras) and Aulus Gratius Potens, soldier of the XXII legion."*

A 3rd-century CE relief from Rome of the god Mithras.

Writing

There were many different languages across the empire. LATIN was used in the west and Greek in the east. Language was important for international trade and government. For many of the new Roman TERRITORIES, this was the first time that writing was used as a form of communication.

PAPER AND PENS

Tools for writing included a wax tablet with two wooden leaves that folded together. Liquid wax was poured into the wax tablet, allowed to harden and written on with the point of a STYLUS. Papyrus, a type of paper from Egypt, was expensive and only used for important documents. The pen would have been made from a reed and the ink was a mixture of soot and olive oil.

This wooden wax tablet, bronze stylus and inkwell date from around 37–68 CE.

> ▶ **Source: Pliny the Elder, Natural History XIII, early 1st century CE**
> Pliny the Elder describes the making of paper from papyrus:
>
> *"… paper is made from the papyrus plant by separating it with a needle point into very thin strips as broad as possible."*

ROMAN ALPHABET

These letters are carved into the base of Trajan's Column in Rome. There were only 22 letters in the Roman alphabet. The Romans did not have the letters W and Y. The letters I and J, U and V, were the same in the Roman alphabet. The Romans also used letters for numbers: I for 1, V for 5, X for 10, L for 50, C for 100, D for 500 and M for 1,000. Roman numerals are sometimes still used on clocks and watches today.

These carved Roman letters appear on Trajan's Column, built in 133 CE, in Rome.

Words to use in your project

communication – *the process of sending information*
correspondence – *letters*
excavate – *to dig up*
language – *a way of speaking or writing*
numerals – *figures denoting numbers*
utensils – *tools*

Glossary

Latin – *the language of ancient Rome*
stylus – *a writing tool, usually made of bronze, used on wax tablets*
territories – *areas under the rule of a single state*

See also: Travel and Trade 12–13; Work and Play 20–21; Living at Home 28–29

CASE STUDY

Writing letters

Vindolanda tablets, from the Vindolanda fort in England, give a snapshot of the life of ordinary Romans. The tablets are made of thinly cut slivers of wood. Letters were written on one side. The wood was then folded in half and the address written on the back.

▶ **Source: Vindolanda tablet 346, 1st–2nd century CE**
One of the first Vindolanda tablets to be translated reads:

"I have sent you ... pairs of socks from Sattua, two pairs of sandals and two pairs of underpants ... I hope that you live in the greatest good fortune."

The Vindolanda tablets are from the 1st and 2nd centuries CE.

Travel and Trade

The wealth of the Roman Empire helped many regions to develop international trade. The East produced wine, fruit and silk; North Africa produced grain; and Gaul and Spain provided olive oil and wine. Roman roads helped to transport the goods.

A 3rd-century CE relief of a ship, from Italy.

ROMAN ROADS

Roman roads are well known for being extremely straight.

The construction of straight roads was something that emperors would boast about and want to be remembered for. Roman roads were built to be very strong and many still exist today. Ermine Street originally ran between London and York in England and is now part of a motorway system.

▶ **Source: Corpus Inscriptionum Latinarum, Vol III No 8, c. 98–117 CE**
A roadside inscription from the reign of Trajan reads:

"The Emperor Caesar Nerva trajan Augustus Germanicus, son of the DEIFIED Nerva, PONTIFEX maximus, holding the TRIBUNICIAN power for the fourth year, father of his country, consul three times, built this road by cutting through mountains and ELIMINATING curves."

A Roman road in Pompeii, Italy.

TRAVELLING BY SEA

The Roman navy patrolled the seas of the empire watching for pirates. Ships often sailed only in the summer, when the weather was calmer, and always close to the land – the Romans had no compasses with which to NAVIGATE.

▶ **Source: Synesius, letter to his brother, c. late 3rd–early 4th century CE**

Synesius wrote this about sea travel:

"For in plain fact the big rollers still kept on, and the sea was at issue with itself. It does this when the wind falls, and the waves it has set going do not fall with it, but, still RETAINING in full force the IMPULSE that started them, meet the onset of the GALE, and to its front oppose their own. Well, when people are sailing in such circumstances, life hangs, as they say, by a slender thread."

Words to use in your project

calculate – *to work out mathematically*
commemorate – *to honour the memory of*
expedition – *a journey*
industry – *business*
nautical – *concerning sailing*
trade – *the act of buying and selling*
traverse – *to travel over*

Glossary

deified – *worshipped as a god*
eliminating – *getting rid of something*
gale – *a gusty wind*
impulse – *a sudden urge*
navigate – *to direct a route*
pontifex – *a member of the principal college of priests*
retaining – *keeping*
steelyard – *a part of a machine used for weighing*
tribunician – *a Roman official chosen by the people to protect their interests*

See also: Writing 10–11; Buildings and Engineering 18–19; Food and Drink 24–25; Dressing Up 26–27

CASE STUDY

Weighing and measuring

Trade became easier when the Romans standardized rules about measuring. This meant that merchants could buy and sell from one another knowing that the way of measuring was the same everywhere. The basic unit of weight in the Roman Empire was the uncia. An uncia was about 27 grams. The Romans sometimes used their denarius coin as a measure of weight.

▶ **Source: Celsus, On Medicine, V.17.1.C, mid-1st century CE**

Around 155 BCE–64 CE, the denarius weighed 4 grams, as described by the writer Celsus:

"… in the ounce there is a weight of 7 denarii."

A 1st-century CE bronze STEELYARD and lead weight.

The Roman Army

Life in the Roman army was tough. Soldiers were killed for sleeping while they were supposed to be on guard. For COWARDICE, a unit was DECIMATED. Yet many still joined the army. After retirement, soldiers were given land and money.

WEAPONS

The ordinary soldier had a spear called a pilum, a dagger called a pugio and a short sword called a gladius. They also wore leather and metal armour. The Romans had giant battering rams, stone-throwing machines and huge crossbows.

> ▶ **Source: Vegetius, Military Science, II.23, c. early 5th century CE**
> A writer from the period described the Roman weaponry:
>
> *"The legion in practice is victorious because of the number of soldiers and the type of machines. First of all, it is equipped with hurling machines which no breastplate, no shield can withstand. For the practice is to have a BALLISTA mounted on a carriage for each century, to each of which are assigned mules and a team of eleven men for loading and firing."*

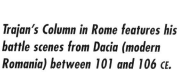

Trajan's Column in Rome features his battle scenes from Dacia (modern Romania) between 101 and 106 CE.

PEOPLE IN THE ARMY

The army was organized into legions of 10,000 men. Foot soldiers were called legionnaires and their leader was the centurion. The centurion wore heavy armour and his helmet had a red plume.

> ▶ **Source: Tacitus, Annals I. xvii, late 1st century CE**
>
> Many soldiers were critical of their superiors, as illustrated in this account of a MUTINY from the 1st century CE:
>
> *"Why should they obey like slaves a few centurions and fewer tribunes, when old men, and many who had lost limbs from wounds, were serving thirty and forty years?"*

This Roman centurion is from a 2nd-century relief from Turin, Italy.

See also: Creation of the Roman Empire 4–5; Rulers and Ruled 6–7; Travel and Trade 12–13; Buildings and Engineering 18–19

CASE STUDY

Walls of defence

Soldiers spent winter months or peacetime in forts, which held between 500–1,000 troops. Every fort had a ditch, a RAMPART and a high stone wall. In the centre of each fort was the principia, or headquarters.

> ▶ **Source: Excerpt from Hadrian's address to a legion based in North Africa, 128 CE**
>
> This quote from the emperor Hadrian praises a legion's wall-building skills:
>
> *"You have built a wall ENTAILING long labour … built of large heavy stones of all sizes … You have cut a trench straight through hard coarse gravel and have made it even by smoothing it."*

This Roman fort was built between 120–138 CE in Cumbria, England.

Death and Burial

During the Roman Empire, people had poor diets, hard living conditions and no modern medicines. Most people did not live past 50 years old and many died at birth. Because death was so much a part of life, the Romans created many funeral rituals.

> ▶ **Source: 12 Tables, Table X.1**
> In about 450 BCE, Roman law ruled that the dead were not allowed to be buried inside the city walls. It stated that:
> *"None is to bury or burn a corpse in the city."*

CEMETERIES

Cemeteries were built near the town gates. This was done for religious reasons but also prevented the spread of disease. The richest Romans were buried in TOMBS along the roadside so that people travelling would remember them. Poorer people could pay for the ashes of relatives to be placed in small spaces in special buildings. The bodies of the poorest members of Roman society and slaves were thrown into large pits.

A Roman urn from the 1st century CE.

This cemetery in Pompeii, Italy, contains many grand tombs.

THE FUNERAL

In the early Roman Empire, CREMATION was common. A CINERARY URN was for the ashes of the dead. Later, Romans buried their dead.

▶ **Source: Polybius, Histories, 53-4.3, 2nd century BCE**

A Roman writer wrote about the funeral of a rich Roman:

"After this, when the burial and the usual rituals have been carried out they place the image of the dead man in the most CONSPICUOUS place in the house, enclosed in a wooded shrine. This image consists of a mask that reproduces his features and COMPLEXION with remarkable faithfulness."

Words to use in your project

afterlife – another life after death
communal – done all together
corpse – a dead body
inhumation – the act of burying a dead body
mourn – to grieve for and remember a dead person
rites – rituals

Glossary

cinerary urn – a container for storing a dead person's ashes
complexion – the tone and texture of skin
conspicuous – very obvious
cremation – the act of burning a dead body before burying or scattering the ashes
River Styx – the river used by the ferryman Charon to transport the dead to the Roman Underworld
tombs – large burial structures, usually for the rich
Underworld – the place where the Roman dead gathered under the earth

See also: Rulers and Ruled 6–7; Religion 8–9; Travel and Trade 12–13; Health 22–23

CASE STUDY

The River Styx

Throughout the period of the Roman Empire, there were different ideas about death. Many believed in an afterlife. Some Romans believed that the dead would be ferried across the RIVER STYX, which led to the UNDERWORLD. A coin was placed in the dead person's mouth to pay the ferrryman.

▶ **Source: Virgil, Aeneid, late 1st century BCE**

Here the journey to the Underworld is described:

"The ferryman there is Charon. Those sailing the waters of the Styx have all been buried. No man may be ferried from fearful bank to fearful bank of this roaring current until his bones are laid to rest."

This coffin detail from 150–180 CE shows the god Hercules at the gates of the Underworld.

Buildings and Engineering

Although the Romans copied many Greek buildings, particularly stadiums and temples, they were the first to use domes and arches. The Romans built with marble from Greece and Italy and were also the first to use concrete.

BUILDING TOOLS

Roman builders used DIVIDERS when they worked with models or drawings of a new building. They used a set square to make sure large blocks of stones would fit together properly. A PLUMB BOB was used to check vertical lines were straight. Good ENGINEERING depended on accurate measurements. A Roman ruler was divided into the basic unit of length, the digitus. The digitus is about 18 mm. There are 16 of these in one pes and five pes makes one passus. One Roman mile was about 1,000 passus.

This 2nd-century CE marble relief shows stonemasons at work.

CARRYING WATER

The job of an AQUEDUCT is to provide a city with a water supply. The water flows along a covered channel at the top of the structure. Roman aqueducts were grand buildings, but they also had a practical purpose.

This is the 1st-century BCE Pont du Gard aqueduct in Nimes, southern France.

▶ **Source: Frontinus, The Supply of Rome II, late 1st century CE**

The importance of aqueducts to Rome is described in the following quote:

"… they are structures of the greatest MAGNITUDE, and … each one carries several CONDUITS; for should it once be necessary to interrupt these, the City would be DEPRIVED of the greater part of its water-supply."

Words to use in your project

frontier – *a border*
implements – *tools*
irrigation – *the supply of water to land or crops*
legacy – *something passed on to people*
pozzolana – *a type of volcanic ash used to make cement*
structures – *buildings*
technology – *the application of scientific knowledge*

Glossary

aqueduct – *a bridge designed for carrying water*
conduits – *channels for water to flow through*
deprived – *denied something*
dividers – *a measuring compass*
engineering – *the science of designing and building things*
magnitude – *great size or importance*
marauding – *attacking and stealing*
mortar – *a building material used for holding bricks together*
plumb bob – *a weight that hangs from a string which is used as a vertical reference point*

See also: Rulers and Ruled 6–7; Travel and Trade 12–13; The Roman Army 14–15

CASE STUDY

Hadrian's Wall

In 122 CE, Emperor Hadrian ordered that a wall be built across the border of northern England to keep out MARAUDING northern tribes. Modern historians believe it took Roman soldiers between six and eight years to build it. It runs for about 120 kilometres. The wall was originally built of earth and wood but was replaced by a stone wall about 10 metres high and 2–3 metres thick. The wall was made from locally available materials such as rubble, MORTAR and stone. To further strengthen the defences, there were forts every thousand paces along the whole length of the wall.

This is a view of Hadrian's Wall in northern England, which was built in the 2nd century CE.

Gladiators

The gladiatorial contest was a popular fight between two men to the death, in front of a huge crowd. It is believed that gladiatorial contests began as part of a funeral ceremony for important people. However, by the time of the emperors, the contests were simply for enjoyment.

GLADIATOR FIGHTS

GLADIATORS were trained in special schools called ludi. They were often slaves and criminals.

If a gladiator survived many fights, he was regarded as a hero and might become famous. At the end of the gladiatorial fight, the emperor decided whether the loser should live. If the emperor wasn't there, the crowds made the decision.

This 1st-century CE mosaic shows a gladiator.

▶ **Source: Pliny the Younger, a panegyric (speech), 100 CE**

Pliny the Younger described being a gladiator:

"Next came a public entertainment – nothing LAX or dissolute to weaken and destroy the manly spirit of his subjects, but one to inspire them to face honourable wounds and look scorn on death, be exhibiting love of glory and desire for victory."

COLOSSEUM

The most spectacular place for gladiatorial contests was the Colosseum in Rome. It could hold over 50,000 people. An AWNING would be stretched across the top to give shade to the onlookers. Below this were cells where the gladiators were kept before being led out to fight. The arena was covered with sand, which could absorb the blood and be swept away easily.

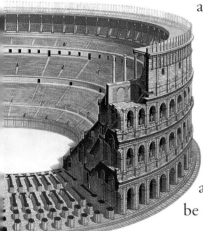

Rome's Colosseum was finished in 80 CE and was used to stage gladiatorial contests.

▶ **Source: Suetonius, Life of Titus, VII.3, First half of the 2nd century CE**

A Roman writer describes a gladiatorial contest:

"… at the dedication of the Colosseum, Titus provided a most LAVISH gladiatorial show."

Words to use in your project

arena – *an area surrounded by seating where events are staged*
auditorium – *the part of a theatre where the audience sits*
condemned – *found guilty*
courageous – *brave*
custom – *a tradition*
glorify – *to strongly admire; worship*
spectacle – *a striking performance or display*

Glossary

awning – *a sheet of canvas stretched over a frame*
exposed – *in full view*
gladiator – *a man trained to fight with weapons against other men or wild animals in an arena*
lavish – *fancy and expensive*
lax – *not very strict*
trident – *a spear with three points at the end*

See also: Rulers and Ruled 6–7; Buildings and Engineering 18–19; Dressing Up 26–27; Pastimes 30–31

CASE STUDY

Gladiator gear

Two types of gladiator were the secutor and the retiarius. The secutor had armour, but this made him very slow and clumsy. The retiarus had only a short tunic but was fast. He used a net to catch his opponent and a TRIDENT to stab him.

▶ **Source: Seneca, Moral Letter 7.2–4, mid-1st century CE**
A Roman writer named Seneca described a contest between two lightly armed gladiators:

"The men have no defensive armour. They are EXPOSED to blows at all points, and no one ever strikes in vain … there is no helmet or shield to deflect the weapon."

A secutor would have worn a helmet like this one, from Pompeii, Italy, 1st century CE.

Health

Many Romans believed that illnesses were caused by curses, witchcraft or punishment from the gods. Therefore, praying at shrines, carrying charms and leaving offerings to the gods were all supposed to help cure an illness. Herbs were used as medicines.

ROMAN TOILETS

The Romans developed a water-supply system that helped to prevent many diseases. Toilets were COMMUNAL and used as places to meet and talk. Underneath the toilets, a stream of water carried away waste. People would then clean themselves with a sponge soaked in vinegar on a stick, which was rinsed in a small stream in front of the toilets.

This 1st-century BCE picture, from Pompeii, Italy, shows warrior Aeneas having an arrowhead removed from his leg.

▶ **Source: Cassius Dio, History of Rome, 49.43.1–4, 3rd century CE**
In 33 BCE, according to Cassius Dio, Emperor Augustus' right-hand man, Marcus Agrippa:

"… cleaned out the sewers, and sailed underground through them to the Tiber".

Roman toilets, such as these from Housesteads Fort on Hadrian's Wall, were built so that a stream of running water could wash away the waste.

DOCTORS

The Romans had no ANAESTHETICS or ANTISEPTICS, so surgery would have been painful and infected wounds would have often led to amputation or death. Doctors tried to heal their patients with herbs.

> ▶ **Source: Galen, Antidotes, 1.1, mid-2nd century CE**
>
> Emperor Marcus Aurelius had a doctor called Galen, who wrote:
>
> *"About Marcus Aurelius I know personally that for his own safety he used to prepare and take each day as much as an Egyptian bean's worth (a small measure) of this ANTIDOTE, swallowing this either with or without a mixture of water or wine or the like. And when he began to get very DROWSY at his daily occupations, he took away the poppy-juice."*

Words to use in your project

administer – *to give a drug*
amputation – *the removal of a limb*
grooming – *the act of looking after your appearance*
sophisticated – *advanced; worldly*
talisman – *a powerful charm*

Glossary

anaesthetics – *drugs given to take away pain before an operation*
antidote – *a cure*
antiseptics – *substances that prevent the growth of germs*
capacious – *spacious*
chatelaine – *a set of short chains attached to a woman's belt*
communal – *done together*
drowsy – *tired*
hygiene – *the conditions related to keeping clean*
Laconian – *relating to an ancient region of Greece*

See also: Death and Burial 16–17; Buildings and Engineering 18–19; Pastimes 30–31

CASE STUDY

Keeping clean

Personal HYGIENE was important to the ancient Romans. Many Romans pinned a CHATELAINE to their clothing, which included tweezers, a fingernail cleaner and an ear cleaner. Visits to the public baths were a regular feature of Roman life.

> ▶ **Source: Lucian, The Bath, 2nd century CE**
>
> Lucian, writing in the 2nd century CE, describes a bathing complex:
>
> *"… CAPACIOUS locker rooms to undress in on each side, with a very high and brilliantly lighted hall in between them, in which are three swimming pools of cold water; it is finished in LACONIAN marble …"*

This Roman chatelaine was pinned to clothing.

Food and Drink

Most Romans ate very little during the day and had a large meal in the evening. For poor Romans their diet was mostly bread, lentils and a small piece of meat. Romans added lots of herbs, spices and sauces to food, including garum – a strong-tasting fish sauce.

A fashionable cup from the 4th century BCE.

HOW THEY COOKED FOOD

The central HEARTH was heated using wood or charcoal. Many emperors were worried about the risk of fire in their cities, so they didn't allow the use of ovens in the home. Poorer Romans relied on buying hot food from street bars called thermapholia.

This stone oven is preserved in the city of Pompeii, Italy.

▶ **Source: Seneca, Moral Letter 41.2, mid-1st century CE**

The Roman writer Seneca described the street bars:

"… the varied cries of the sausage dealer and CONFECTIONER and of all the PEDDLERS of the cook shops, HAWKING their wares, each with his own peculiar INTONATION."

Cooking was usually done in saucepans made of bronze because they cooked the food more evenly.

DRINKS

Wealthy Romans drank from glass cups, while ordinary Romans used pottery cups. Most Romans drank wine, adding water, herbs and honey.

> ▶ **Source: Pliny the Younger, Letters, II.6, early 2nd century CE**
>
> Pliny the Younger describes how a host gave different qualities of wine to different guests:
>
> *"He had even put the wine into tiny little FLASKS, divided into three categories, not with the idea of giving his guests the opportunity of choosing, but to make it impossible for them to refuse what they were given. One lot was intended for himself and for us, another for his lesser friends (all his friends are graded) and the third for his and our freedmen."*

Words to use in your project

banquet – *a feast*
condiments – *substances used for flavouring food*
culinary – *related to cooking*
dilute – *to add water; make weaker*
etiquette – *polite behaviour*
indulged – *enjoyed or satisfied*
neat – *no water added (to a drink)*

Glossary

confectioner – *a person who sells sweets*
flasks – *containers for liquid*
hawking – *selling goods in the streets*
hearth – *the floor of or area around a fireplace*
intonation – *the rise and fall of the voice when speaking*
peddlers – *salespersons*
unique – *special or original*

See also: Travel and Trade 12–13; Health 22–23; Living at Home 28–29

CASE STUDY

Bowls and Plates

In the 1st and 2nd centuries CE, it was fashionable for rich Romans to eat from a glossy red pottery called Samian ware. Samian ware was made in large factories in Italy and Gaul.

> ▶ **Source: Gaius Petronius, Satyricon, late 1st century CE**
>
> A 1st-century writer named Gaius Petronius mocked a rich man who boasted about the quality of his plates and glasses:
>
> *"Perhaps you're wondering why I am UNIQUE in owning Corinthian plates? Because, of course, the dealer I buy it from is named Corinthus."*

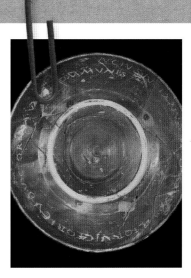

A Samian-ware plate from the 3rd century CE.

Dressing Up

Romans were fashion conscious and made sure they had fine clothes, jewellery, hairstyles and make-up. Fashions changed over time – in the early empire men had long hair and beards, but later on it was fashionable to have short hair and be clean-shaven.

THE CLOTHES THEY WORE

For everyday wear both men and women wore light tunics, but on special occasions they wore TOGAS. Both togas and TUNICS were single pieces of cloth that were fastened at the shoulder with a brooch or pin. Light colours were the most popular. On their feet, both men and women wore sandals. When a state was conquered by the Romans, the people often adopted the Roman style of dress.

▶ **Source: Tacitus, Agricola, 21, 97–8 CE**

Tacitus, in his account of his father-in-law Agricola's governorship of Britain, described the Roman influence:

"… even our style of dress came in to favour and the toga was everywhere to be seen [in Britain]."

This 1st-century BCE FUNERARY MOSAIC shows a man in a white toga.

ROMAN JEWELLERY

Women wore a lot of jewellery, including rings set with gemstones and pearls. Both men and women wore rings and sometimes had them on all ten fingers. The wealthiest Romans also wore CAMEOS set into rings and PENDANTS. A cameo normally showed people, gods or mythological figures.

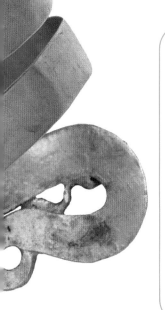

A gold amulet from the 1st century CE, found in Pompeii, Italy.

> ▶ **Source: Juvenal, Satire VI, late 1st–early 2nd century CE**
>
> The poet Juvenal wrote about the way wealthy women dressed up in jewellery:
>
> *"There is nothing that a woman will not permit herself to do, nothing that she deems shameful, when she encircles her neck with green emeralds, and fastens huge pearls to her ELONGATED ears: there is nothing more INTOLERABLE than a wealthy woman."*

Words to use in your project

adorned – *decorated*
appearance – *the way something looks*
cosmetics – *make-up*
fashionable – *stylish*

Glossary

cameos – *portraits in profile carved on a background of a different colour*
complexion – *the tone and texture of the skin*
elongated – *stretched*
funerary mosaic – *artwork made to honour someone who has died*
intolerable – *unable to endure*
ochre – *a pale brown or yellow mineral made of clay*
pendants – *necklaces*
togas – *loose, flowing pieces of clothing*
tunics – *pieces of clothing made of thin material without sleeves and reaching the knee*

See also: Creation of the Roman Empire 4–5; Writing 10–11; Gladiators 20–21

CASE STUDY

Make-up grinders

Make-up grinders were used to crush minerals for make-up. Rich Roman women used make-up whenever they were going out in public. It was fashionable to have a pale COMPLEXION because it showed that you did not have to go outdoors to work. Faces were painted white with chalk or white lead and cheeks and lips were coloured red using OCHRE or the sediment from red wine. The eyebrows and edges of the eyes were made black with ash. Make-up was stored in small pots and bottles.

A small 1st-century CE make-up grinder, found in Britain.

Living at Home

Most Roman houses were small and low quality. In cities, most people lived in flats called tenements. These were several stories high and had no running water or SANITATION. Wealthier Romans could afford a town house and a VILLA in the country.

ROMAN HOUSES

Most Roman villas followed the same design. The first room was the hallway, or ATRIUM. The atrium had an opening in the roof and a pool. This helped to keep the house cool in summer. Romans preferred little furniture and rich decorations on the walls and floor. In other parts of the Roman Empire, villas varied and copied local tastes.

This is a view from the outside of a Roman villa in Herculaneum, Italy.

▶ **Source: Pliny the Younger, letter to his friend, late 1st–early 2nd century CE**
The younger Pliny boasts to a friend of 'the charm of his Laurentine villa' in Italy, saying that:

"... the villa is spacious enough for my needs, and the upkeep is not expensive."

DECORATING THE HOUSE

The floors of wealthy Romans were decorated with MOSAICS, many of which have survived. This form of home decoration was practised in Egypt and was adopted by the Romans. The scenes on mosaics were of legends or daily life. Interior walls of villas were decorated with FRESCOES, picturing myths. Rich Romans also had outdoor scenes painted on the walls so that they looked like views from a window.

This mosaic of a man drinking is from the 1st century CE.

See also: Religion 8–9; Buildings and Engineering 18–19; Food and Drink 24–25; Pastimes 30–31

CASE STUDY

Keeping warm

Villas in the northern parts of the Roman Empire kept warm with an underfloor central-heating system called a hypocaust. A fire was lit next to an outside wall and was kept going by a slave. The heat would be drawn into an open space under the floor and rise into the walls. These hypocausts can be seen in many Roman buildings, particularly in Pompeii.

▶ **Source: Pliny the Younger, Letter II.17, late 1st–early 2nd century CE**

Pliny the Younger described the use of heating to keep his villa warm:

"Attached to this is a bedroom connected to a passageway with a hollow floor and walls fitted with pipes from which it receives hot air circulated in all directions at a healthful temperature."

This hypocaust from the 1st century BCE is from the Gallo-Roman town of Alesia in France.

Pastimes

All Romans, with the exception of slaves, were given holidays. Originally, these were days that celebrated religious festivals, but over time they lost their meaning. In the reign of Claudius, 159 days each year were holidays, but by the 5th century CE, this had risen to 200 days.

The public baths in the English city of Bath.

THEATRE

Many Roman towns had an open-air theatre. These were usually SEMI-CIRCULAR in shape.

Most of the plays performed were Greek or written by Romans in the Greek style. Roman theatre-goers preferred comedies. The Romans also invented two new forms of theatre – mime and PANTOMIME.

▶ **Source: Fronto, Elements of History, XVII, 2nd century CE**
The importance of theatre is described by an early imperial Roman writer:

"… it was the height of political wisdom for the emperor not to neglect even actors and other performers of the stage, circus and the arena, since he knew that the Roman people is held fast by two things above all, the grain supply and the theatrical shows."

This mosaic of a tragic theatre mask was created in the 1st century CE.

THE BATHS

Romans went to the public baths to get clean, meet friends, exercise with weights or to play ball and board games.

> ▶ **Source: Seneca, Moral Letter 41.1–2, mid–1st century** CE
>
> The Roman writer Seneca gave a useful description of Roman baths:
>
> *"When the stronger fellows are exercising and swinging heavy laden weights in their hands, when they are working hard or pretending to be working hard, I hear their groans … Add to this the arrest of a BRAWLER or a thief, and the fellow who always likes to hear his own voice in the bath, and those who jump into the pool with a mighty splash as they strike the water."*

Words to use in your project

festivities – *fun celebrations*
patron – *a person who gives financial or other support*
performance – *acting or playing music*
popular – *liked by many people*
vulgar – *lacking class or good taste*

Glossary

abide – *to put up with*
brawler – *someone who is in a fight*
corruption – *acting dishonestly for money or personal gain*
dregs – *the most worthless parts*
fraction – *a part of a whole*
lingo – *a foreign language*
pantomime – *a piece of drama or poetry with music and dance*
semi-circular – *one half of a circle*

See also: Religion 8–9; Gladiators 20–21; Health 22–23; Living at Home 28–29

CASE STUDY

The god of music

The god Apollo was the patron of music. But for wealthy Romans, music was seen as something that was beneath them.

> ▶ **Source: Juvenal, Satire III, 58, late 1st–early 2nd** CE
>
> The Roman writer Juvenal complained that listening or dancing to music could lead to CORRUPTION as it was associated with Greek luxury:
>
> *"I cannot ABIDE a Rome of Greeks; and yet what FRACTION of our DREGS comes from Greece? The Syrian Orontes has long since poured into the Tiber, bringing with it its LINGO and its manners, its flutes and its slanting harp-strings."*

This 2nd-century CE statue of the Roman god of music, Apollo, is from Cyrene in Libya.

Index

Ancient Rome Timeline

753 BCE
The city of Rome is founded by twin brothers Romulus and Remus (according to Roman mythology).

509 BCE
The republic of Rome is established after the Etruscans are driven out.

450 BCE
The Romans establish their first written laws called the 12 Tables.

390 BCE
The Gauls invade Italy and are defeated by the Romans.

300–400 BCE
The Romans are exposed to Greek ideas. They begin to worship Greek gods and goddesses, but they give them Roman names.

140s BCE
Rome gains control of North Africa, Spain, Greece, Macedonia and part of Turkey.

60s BCE
Rome conquers eastern Asia Minor, Syria and Judea under the direction of General Pompey.

58–51 BCE
Julius Caesar conquers Gaul (modern France).

49 BCE
Caesar invades Italy, starting a civil war.

44 BCE
Caesar is assassinated by a group of senators who hope to restore the Roman republic. Civil war breaks out again.

43 BCE
Mark Antony fights for control of Rome – seeking help from Cleopatra, queen of Egypt. They fall in love.

30 BCE
Rome conquers Egypt.

27 BCE
Augustus becomes the first emperor of Rome. His rule marks the period we know as Pax Romana (Roman Peace). It lasts for about 200 years.

30 CE
Jesus Christ is believed to have been crucified by the Romans for treason. However, his followers begin to spread Christianity throughout the Roman Empire.

43 CE
Emperor Claudius invades Britain.

200s CE
The Goths, a Germanic tribe, invade the Roman Empire on numerous occasions.

Late 300s CE
Christianity becomes the official religion of the empire.

Early 400s CE
Germanic tribes invade Spain, Gaul (now France) and North Africa.

410 CE
The Visigoths invade and loot Rome.

476 CE
The last Roman emperor is overthrown.